The
Dictionary
of
High School
B.S.

First published in 2008 by
Zest Books, an imprint of Orange Avenue Publishing
35 Stillman Street, Suite 121, San Francisco, CA 94107
www.zestbooks.net

Created and produced by Zest Books, San Francisco, CA
© 2008 by Orange Avenue Publishing LLC
Illustrations © 2008 by Michael Miller

Typeset in Dante and Pinch

Teen Nonfiction / Humor / Reference

Library of Congress Control Number: 2008925994
ISBN-13: 978-0-9790173-9-1
ISBN-10: 0-9790173-9-4

CREDITS
EDITORIAL DIRECTOR: Karen Macklin
CREATIVE DIRECTOR: Hallie Warshaw
WRITER: Lois Beckwith
EDITOR: Karen Macklin
ILLUSTRATOR: Michael Miller
COVER DESIGN: Debbie Berne Design, Oakland, CA
PRODUCTION ARTIST: Cari McLaughlin
TEEN ADVISORY BOARD: Carolyn Hou, Lisa Macklin, Maxfield J. Peterson,
                     Joe Pinsker, Hannah Shr

Printed in China
First printing, 2008
10 9 8 7 6 5 4 3 2 1

*Every effort has been made to ensure that the information presented is accurate. Readers
are strongly advised to read product labels, follow manufacturers' instructions, and heed
warnings. The publisher disclaims any liability for injuries, losses, untoward results, or
any other damages that may result from the use of the information in this book.*

The
Dictionary
of
High School
B.S.

FROM ACNE TO VARSITY,
ALL THE FUNNY, LAME, AND ANNOYING ASPECTS
OF HIGH SCHOOL LIFE

LOIS BECKWITH

Sure, **high school** has its high points. Among them: acing a test, having your first real **relationship**, actually learning something, and — of course — leaving. But it's also full of ridiculous rules, irritating people, and

ongoing drama — in other words, a ton of B.S. that you have to deal with *every* day. Now, finally, there's a book about it.

In this uncensored dictionary, you'll find straight talk about all of your favorite and not-so-favorite aspects of high school. Broken down for you in handy A-to-Z fashion, this little guidebook gives the lowdown on everything from **substitute teachers**, **school shrinks**, and **prom** to **hooking up**, **making out**, and the highly anticipated (though who knows why, really) Sweet 16. You'll read dozens of entries on the stuff you stress over daily—like your boyfriend or girlfriend, college applications, and AP classes—plus get an inside look at the B.S. that comes along with even the things you love, like parties and summer break.

Of course, we couldn't include *all* the annoying, lame, and funny aspects of high school (as advertised on the front cover)—that would be kind of impossible. But you're certain to uncover a fair load of bull and (hopefully) an equal load of amusement. And that's really the point, isn't it? Because when all the B.S. starts to get you down, there's only one thing to do: Laugh in its face.

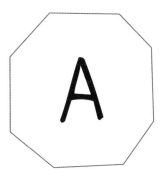

acne (n) also known as zits. **1.** facial eruptions that are simultaneously infuriating, fascinating, and gross. **2.** a massive source of embarrassment, especially when the bumps are huge, red, and resistant to benzoyl peroxide and concealer, the latter of which just makes them worse and, ironically, more noticeable. **3.** a personal affect that will leave your friends assuring you "It's not that noticeable" before your big date, but they're probably lying; everyone notices it, but they don't care as much as you do.

after school (n) **1.** the time between your last class of the day and dinner. **2.** an interim during which any number of things can happen, such as going to sports practice or school play rehearsal, studying, watching cable, eating junk food at a friend's house, making out with your boyfriend or girlfriend while you're supposed to be studying, updating your MySpace/Facebook page, or just hanging out. **3.** an ominous threat, indicating your butt will be kicked at that time (as in "See you after school").

all-nighter

alcohol (n) **1.** an intoxicating liquid in the form of beer, wine, or hard liquor such as gin, vodka, or rum. **2.** a substance many kids consider an essential element of a good **party** and therefore go to great lengths to obtain, opting to either steal it from **parents**, ask an older sibling (or some random person on the street) to buy it for them, or attempt to purchase it with a **fake ID**. **3.** the cause of countless teenagers getting wasted, **hooking up**, puking, doing something they will later regret, getting **grounded**, or all of the above.

all-nighter (n) **1.** the experience of staying up all night. **2.** a frantic evening spent **studying** for an exam in a subject that one knows nothing about; includes the slamming down of Red Bull, coffee, and/or junk food while attempting (in vain) to read one's handwriting from two months ago, desperately calling friends for help to understand obscure concepts, profiling the **teacher** in an effort to divine the material he or she will include on the test, and strategically skimming *A Tale of Two Cities* (or similar material). **3.** *alternate use*: a night spent socializing—i.e., partying, watching **movies**, or playing video games —until one is so sleep-deprived that he or she can't see straight or is suffering the shakes.

AP classes (n) abbreviation for advanced placement **classes**. **1.** courses on subjects ranging from history to **biology** to the rarely spoken Latin that **smart** and/or ambitious kids take to earn **college** credits before even entering college. **2.** classes that culminate with the dreaded AP tests, which are graded in a somewhat mysterious and maddening way, especially because they often include an essay component for which one earns a score of 1–5 — without ever really knowing why one got that score. **3.** classes for which students are often promised college credit only to later find out that the college they selected won't give credit for any of the AP courses they took. *See also* IB classes.

assembly (n) **1.** a convocation of the entire student body, usually in the school gym or auditorium. **2.** an event, usually characterized by a zoo-like atmosphere with lots of yelling, flirting, and maybe even crowd surfing, that features the appearance of the principal and/or the discussion of something supposedly so important it requires everyone getting together in the same space; event may feature a talk about the rise in campus violence, a lecture on drunk driving, or a performance by a visiting African dance troupe.

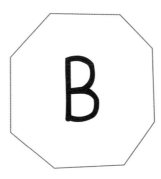

babysitting (v) **1.** watching other people's kids for money; involves two phases: the part when the kids are awake and one can't channel surf, watch cable, call friends, or raid the parents' fridge, and the part when the kids are asleep and one can do pretty much whatever as long as no evidence is left behind. **2.** employing a great excuse to not do homework while still positioning oneself as a responsible person and making some cash. **3.** for older siblings, doing an annoying task for no pay and, frustratingly, at the expense of one's social life.

backpack (n) **1.** a container for all of your crap. **2.** a kind of geeky, and sometimes painfully heavy, appendage that people often try to make cooler by posing with it over one shoulder. **3.** a place with "secret" inside pockets, in which one may try to hide things from nosy parents.

back-to-school shopping (v) **1.** purchasing tons of stuff, from school supplies to new clothes, in preparation for the coming school year. (n) **2.** a carefully orchestrated marketing scheme by the industries that stand to make a buck off of the idea that students need all new stuff every September. **3.** a shopping season that can start as early as July, when no one should even be thinking about school. **4.** a chance to score some cool new clothes on Dad's dime and assemble the perfect portfolio of color-coordinated folders, notebooks, and binders, which will only get trashed days later.

band (n) *rock*: **1.** a group of people who play instruments and sing, typically in a somewhat public forum. **2.** a musical group formed by people with sometimes little musical talent, as the point of being in a band is not always to play music, but often to simply say that one is in a band.

3. for guys, a group to join to potentially get more action; for girls, a group to join in order to wear cute clothes on stage and seem kind of badass. *school*: **1.** a school-sanctioned group made up of players of trumpets, flutes, clarinets, drums, and other instruments. **2.** the anti-cool version of a rock band in which one is required to actually practice one's instrument, participate in painful, frequently off-key fall and spring concerts, and don geeky wool uniforms on 90-degree days for the purpose of marching in a local parade. **3.** a channel through which one may get to play in the Macy's Thanksgiving Day Parade, if one's band is really good (although this may also require dreaded fundraising).

baseball hat guys (n)
1. boys who have baseball caps seemingly glued to their heads; the hats scream the name of a university and/or sports team (e.g., UCLA lacrosse, UVM coed naked beer pong) and their bills have been aggressively folded. **2.** popular party dudes or jocks who react with exasperation when teachers ask that the hats be removed during class.

baseball hat guy

bases (n) **1.** a sports-inspired metaphor for the progressive stages of intimate relations between people: "first" is French kissing, "second" is groping above the waist, "third" is getting your hand down someone's pants, and "home run" really needs no explanation, does it? **2.** a sexual innuendo (probably invented by a totally insensitive jock) that is so old that even most parents and grandparents know what it means. *See also* hooking up, making out, *and* sex.

bathroom (n) **1.** the place where one goes to do one's business. **2.** the locale for applying makeup, gossiping, and providing cover when cutting class, crying, or smoking. **3.** a prime location for fights. **4.** the home of the grossest soap and scratchiest paper towels around. **5.** a canvas for the most inspired and revealing graffiti anywhere in the school.

bell (n) **1.** an alarming, loud, and shrill noise used to signal the beginning and end of class periods.

2. a sound of liberation when it identifies the end of class, but a sound of dread when it identifies the beginning (specifically if one is running late to class, or not en route at all).

best friend (n) **1.** one's closest companion with whom one does and shares everything. **2.** one-half of a pair of friends who've become merged in people's minds, as the two are never seen apart (e.g., Jackie and Suzie are also known as Jackuzie). **3.** a favorite companion who can stir feelings of anxiety and possessiveness if that companion is the type who believes a person can really have only one best friend (after all, either you're the best or you're not, right?).
4. sometimes someone of the opposite gender for which one needs to constantly suffer other people's "When are you going to just go out already?" comments.
5. a person one may never speak to again if he or she hooks up with one's long-time crush or befriends a mutually despised clique.

biology class (n) **1.** the place where the most entertaining science is taught. **2.** a class that includes the dissection of frogs and the study of human anatomy, as well as the potential diseases and disorders that could develop if said human anatomy does not function properly. **3.** a class that involves working with a lab partner, who may be a best friend or a major crush (making biology really fun but not very useful) or some random annoying person (making the class complete torture).

bitch

bitch (n) **1.** an unnecessarily mean **girl** who regularly engages in spreading **rumors** and **gossip**, **lies** with ease, and takes great pleasure in humiliating, making fun of, and excluding people. **2.** a popular girl who is part of a reigning **clique**, or someone who is **insecure** and has a lot of issues. **3.** the girl who plays nice when she wants something, then acts totally distant or cruel as soon as she gets it. **4.** the female version of the **jerk**, who she may in fact date. **5.** you, when you're having a bad day.

blackboard (n) 1. a huge surface that a teacher writes on with chalk in order to conduct lessons. 2. a giant and unattractive structure that sits *behind* your teacher, but seems to be *in front* of you for about 80 percent of your life. 3. a board that was likely named for its original color, but is often actually green. 4. the source of a terrible noise if someone uses chalk too passionately or drags their fingernails across it. 5. a canvas for uninspired graffiti and stupid comments.

blog (n) 1. from weblog; an online publication or journal of postings in reverse chronological order, the quality of which ranges from worthwhile to dumb and incredibly boring. 2. a vehicle of self-expression written by some kid who has no concept of "too much information" and posts really bad poetry or personal revelations. 3. a great medium for gossip, political debate (if one is into that kind of thing), and photos of celebrities in compromising positions. 4. a total time suck, and thus an effective procrastination tool. 5. when vaguely compelling and picked up by the media, a ticket to (probably short-lived) fame.

breasts (n) 1. the fatty tissue housing mammary glands. 2. the things girls have that straight boys obsess and fantasize about. 3. when of a large size, the focus of a lot of attention from guys, which may also make the owner of said objects extremely uncom-fortable and wishing for smaller versions (an idea that many small-chested girls can't even begin to comprehend).

boyfriend/girlfriend (n)
1. a person to whom one is attached in a romantic way and with whom one has some kind of ongoing relationship. **2.** a willing make-out partner. **3.** often thought of as the key to one's happiness, though in reality this is not always the case. **4.** a nice thing to have when prom time comes around, but otherwise not necessary. **5.** a stressor in life if the relationship is not going well; a nice thing to have if you are in love.

boys (n) also known as guys. **1.** people possessing certain biological equipment. **2.** those who are fueled largely by the massive amounts of testosterone pulsing through their bloodstream (yes, even the sensitive, poetry-digging guys). **3.** those who (due to number 2) are obsessed with the idea of sex, as well as doing things that are pretty dangerous like skateboarding down mall escalators, jumping off high roofs for the hell of it, playing football, and even beating the crap out of each other. **4.** people who are unclear on the concept of how to relate to girls, which can lead to behavior that puzzles girls to no end, such as not calling, ignoring, teasing, and running away.

bra (n) **1.** an undergarment worn by girls to support and lift their breasts, and to prevent their nipples from showing through their shirts. **2.** a source of tremendous fantasy for young males who want to get their hands on what's underneath. **3.** a source of tremendous anxiety for young males who have no idea how one actually removes these straightjacket-like devices with any kind of finesse. **4.** a source of tremendous annoyance for

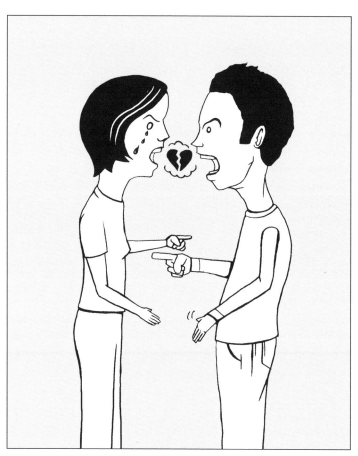

breakup

girls whose breasts are either too small or too big to fit into the bras that actually look cute. **5.** a somewhat irritating, embarrassing, and at times painful thing to shop for, especially when one's mother likes to comment on "how much you've grown!" and gets extremely suspicious when one shows interest in a bra that could be even remotely sexy.

breakup (n) **1.** a parting of ways between people romantically involved. **2.** a devastating, world-collapsing event that often includes crying, being depressed, and talking to friends ad nauseam about the misery of the situation. **3.** an event that often leads to the use of revenge-inspired tactics such as spreading vicious rumors and publicly making out with a cute guy or hot girl at a party. **4.** an almost inevitable product of heading off to college. **5.** an event that is the worst when it takes place right before Valentine's Day or the prom. **6.** for some couples, a regularly occurring (and for friends, increasingly tiresome) event alternating with getting back together.

break up (v) **1.** to sever ties with a significant other because he or she cheated on you, flirted with your best friend, and/or refused to *ever* pay when you went out.

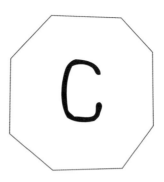

car (n) **l.** a vehicle one may legally drive once hitting age 16, 17, or 18 (depending on state laws) **2.** a sweet chariot of liberty that—especially if one buys it with one's own money—enables freedom of movement and independence from parents. **3.** a chick magnet for guys and a user magnet for people who always "need a ride." **4.** a super prime retreat for making out and rounding the bases, if parked in the right place. **5.** a tool of manipulation for parents who permit its use only in accordance with good behavior. **6.** for a lucky few, a gift in recognition of scoring a 4.0 GPA, getting into a fancy college, or turning "Sweet 16." **7.** for the majority of teens, a loud, noisy, puttering 10-year-old Chevy or Dodge (but even that beats being driven around by parents).

Catholic school (n) **l.** a private, religious educational facility to which parents must pay tuition to send their kids, and where students have to wear uniforms and are taught by priests and nuns.

2. a place where parents will often send their offspring to shield them from evils such as alcohol, drugs, and sex, even though, in reality, Catholic school kids tend to party way harder than their public school counterparts.

cell phone (n) **1.** a lifeline to everyone. **2.** a device used to text anyone and everyone during class, although some teachers will confiscate phones at times, which is a huge buzz kill. **3.** a subtle form of control by parents who know that, thanks to this device, they can reach their kids at all times.

chalk (n) **1.** a writing instrument for a blackboard. **2.** the substance that finds its way all over the hands, faces, and, in the most unfortunate (yet hilarious) scenarios, butts of absentminded teachers.

cheating (v) **1.** to use devious tactics to score higher than you should on a test, exam, or pop quiz. **2.** to employ deception, including looking at the smart kid's answers while taking a test, getting the answers to a test ahead of time, bringing a cheat sheet into an exam, cobbling together an essay from stuff found online (also known as "plagiarism"), and enlisting a friend who took the class a year before to play ghostwriter. **3.** to take a big risk, because getting caught is at the very least embarrassing and actually quite serious if one gets suspended or, in really bad cases, is refused admission to college.

cheerleader (n) **1.** a perky rooter for school sports teams who can produce school spirit on demand; mostly girls, but in some hard-core Midwest states also guys who tend to be built and can toss girls a bunch of feet into the air. **2.** girls who — due to unavoidable constant proximity — frequently end up dating the jocks on the assorted teams they support. **3.** although sometimes dismissed as trivial chicks in cute outfits with pom-poms — or even as bitches — girls who are frequently just as cool as alternative girls and generally better dancers. **4.** girls who come in two different varieties: the ones from kind of rich or suburban schools (pretty, highly gymnastic girls in full makeup sporting high ponytails) or the ones from grittier public schools (badass chicks wearing enormous hoop earrings who bust it out on the court/field and may even krump); needless to say, the meeting of these two types at a game is a delight to behold.

chess club (n) **1.** a school group whose members sit around and play chess, and perhaps enter citywide competitions of the game. **2.** a fellowship of super brainy, and often geeky, kids; they know everyone thinks they're geeks, but they don't care because they (a) belong to and take pride in their own kind of geek gang and (b) know they will likely go to Harvard or Stanford, and therefore don't really sweat the popularity contest thing.

class (n) also known as classroom **1.** the actual physical place where a student learns. **2.** the people one studies alongside and will eventually graduate from high school with (if all goes as planned). **3.** the pool of folks one will see at a reunion 20 years down the line, at which point a random make-out session could take place with an even more random classmate who is now hot, rich, or simply still single.

class clown (n) **1.** the quintessential jokester who is usually a guy and compensating for less-than-stellar looks with a sense of humor in hopes of scoring with the girls. **2.** a big attention-seeking loudmouth who will end up as a successful car salesman. **3.** a big attention-seeking loudmouth who will end up as the next Jerry Seinfeld.

class ring (n) **1.** a piece of jewelry that commemorates one's high school years, often personalized with the buyer's birthstone, initials, and all kinds of symbols indicating areas of interest or academic achievement (from drama club to the National Honor Society, rollerblading, skateboarding, and/or NASCAR).

2. the symbol of a ridiculously expensive and kind of dumb tradition that just won't die. **3.** a waste of money, because after the initial euphoria of having one wears off, one will soon wonder why he or she even bothered to buy it.

class ring

class superlatives (n) **1.** categorizations of select outgoing seniors who are recognized by fellow students (who actually vote on these things) as excelling in a particular area. **2.** awards given to people who are "the most" or "est" something (e.g., most likely to succeed, cutest, most full of B.S.). **3.** titles that can later function as major letdowns when "most likely to succeed" winds up in prison, "cutest class couple" ends up in divorce court, and "biggest flirt" becomes a porn star or an 800-pound recluse.

class trip (n) **1.** an excursion taken en masse by a group of students. **2.** a kind of a last hurrah for graduating seniors. **3.** a trip that usually involves some sort of amusement park as the central activity even though the important events (generally drinking alcohol and hooking up) happen on the bus and in the hotel, if it's an overnight trip. **4.** a time when cliques, bitchiness, fights, and maybe even crying come into play. **5.** a much-needed respite from parents that seems to end way too soon.

clique (n) **1.** an exclusive tribe of individuals who hang out together all the time. **2.** a mini gang made up of members who derive almost as much pleasure from excluding others as they do from being glued to each other. **3.** a hotbed for bitter fighting among members, several of whom may actually hate each other but don't dare sever ties for fear of social isolation and sitting alone at lunch.

clothes (n) **1.** the things one wears to avoid going naked. **2.** an important tool of self-expression. **3.** items subject to the whims of fashion, which means that those high-waisted capri pants or the bomber jacket from last year may now be totally stupid looking. **4.** a means of rebellious expression for punks, emos, goths, drama club members, and assorted too-cool-for-school individuals who opt out of mall culture altogether, and shop exclusively at vintage stores and places like the Salvation Army. **5.** something that rich kids buy a lot of only to throw away once the fashion is out (two weeks later) and start all over again.

club (n) **1.** a school-sanctioned group, the members of which are all into the same thing. **2.** just another thing to put on a college application. **3.** a crappy thing to be a part of when it comes to the inevitable, annual fund-raising.

coach (n) **1.** an adult who provides guidance, training, and supervision for a sports team. **2.** someone who seemingly leads a team because he or she loves it, but who really does it because that person gets paid extra for it. **3.** in some cases, the only person you feel comfortable going to about something that's bothering you. **4.** in other cases, a real hard-ass who makes a habit of yelling, expressing bitter disappointment, and being generally pissed. **5.** a combination of numbers 3 and 4.

college (n) **1.** an institution of higher education. **2.** the destination many people feel is the sole purpose for enduring high school. **3.** the reason some students participate in several dozen extracurricular activities and stress over every B+. **4.** a lesser concern for students who set their sights on the local community college, which is sort of college lite (but, in fact, is also a lot cheaper than an academic powerhouse and is easy to transfer out of in a couple of years). **5.** the easiest and fastest way for most to get out of their hometown and away from their parents.

college application (n)
1. a series of documents —including transcript, SAT scores, and a dreaded essay—that students submit to attempt gaining admission to college.
2. a package of crap that is torture to assemble and forces a student to rethink all those grades earned over the past 3-plus years.
3. when in the form of the "common application," one basic application that can be sent to a number of schools; because so many kids apply to these particular schools, this less complex application doesn't require documenting how one's dog's death came to reveal the meaning of life and led to the opening of a canine medical center, which is kind of refreshing.

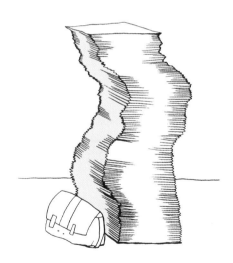

college application

college fair (n) **1.** an assembly (usually held in the cafeteria or **gym**) of marketing people and alums from dozens of educational institutions. **2.** a gathering of **college** sales reps who hype their school and try to entice aspiring college students to go there (even if it's impossible to make the cut), and to get **parents** to pay huge sums of money to send a kid there (even if they can't afford it). **3.** the primary source of an eventual onslaught of mail. **4.** an extensive display of glossy pamphlets filled with photos of happy, culturally diverse students hanging out on autumnal campuses; serious, yet charismatic-looking professors; and art students (think filmmakers and ballerinas). **5.** a place to learn about college financial aid (loans with huge inter-est rates) and **scholarships** because a higher education is so ridiculously expensive.

college visits (n) **1.** trips made, with one or both **parents**, to schools one is considering attending. **2.** a whirlwind tour of a region of the United States, such as the Northeast or Midwest, or perhaps to just one city, like Boston, where there are approximately 543 schools of higher learning. **3.** an exhausting excursion that may include staying in really cheap motels or with some long-lost aunt. **4.** a stop at a **college** campus that includes requisite activities like the campus tour (led by a perky student who is not really representative of the people who go there) as well as the information session (which is so boring you have to keep shaking your parents to keep them awake, or vice versa). **5.** an opportunity to see other freaked-out **juniors** and **seniors** from all over the country (some of whom are kind of hot), as well as their

copycat

parents (who all look kind of tired). **6.** an opportunity to get a sweatshirt emblazoned with the school's name, which could be cool or a fashion disaster, depending on that school's colors.

cool (adj) **1.** a mysterious, amorphous, highly desirable quality that makes anyone, or anything that exudes it, very appealing. **2.** a characteristic that is in part defined by trying really hard to *not* look like one is trying to impress anyone at all. **3.** a word that parents and teachers somehow manage to use wrong or too much, which makes the things they're describing sound anything but cool.

cops (n) also known as pigs, 5-0, and po-po. **1.** members of law enforcement who, if you go to a really rough school, may be on hand in case anything goes down. **2.** the people to avoid if one is cutting class, hanging out on the beach at 3 am (when it's no doubt closed), driving around without a license, or raging at a house party. **3.** adults who seem scary when they first approach you, but then often say things like, "You don't have to go home, you just have to leave here," or, "We won't do anything this time, but don't let it happen again," because they were once young, too, and unless you are doing something *really* crazy, they just don't care that much.

copycat (n) **1.** a person who not so subtly absorbs the personal style of another person, much to the first person's irritation. **2.** an extraordinarily insecure person who unfortunately has yet to define and discover any real sense of self, and therefore will show up to school wearing the exact pair of kick-ass boots you just bought, while also denying that he or she knew you had them.

crush (n) **1.** a completely out-of-control, anguish-causing longing and affection for someone that is often unrequited and even sometimes unnoticed. **2.** a delicious and intoxicating condition that is also perhaps slightly masochistic, especially when said longing is for a best friend, a friend's sibling, a much older or younger person, or someone who is just plain wrong. **3.** a condition that may involve endless daydreaming, countless hours on the phone boring a friend with scenarios of what might happen, and feeling very, very uncool after any kind of contact with the crush-ee. **4.** a situation that may involve finding out in the last weeks of one's senior year, when it's kind of too late to get

together, that the feeling was mutual.

crying (v) **1.** the act of tears forming in, and falling from, one's eyes. (n) **2.** a common occurrence on high school grounds brought on by breakups, fights, failed tests, broken nails, and more.(n) **3.** a much more frequent occurrence among girls, who are said to be more emotional than boys; the truth is that lots of boys are just as emotional, but societal rules don't permit them to cry (except when they're on the football team and lose the championship or snap their leg in two on the field).

curfew (n) **1.** the time, typically determined by one's parents, at which one must be home, whether it's from a date, hanging out with friends, going to the movies, or anything else fun. **2.** a deadline that seems to come up after what feels like 45 minutes. **3.** something that when not followed usually results in getting grounded.

cutting class (v) **1.** to not go to class. **2.** what one does to avoid a test one didn't study for, ditch a class that is extremely boring, or simply get out of school for the day. **3.** a high school "crime" that has repercussions ranging from the notification of one's parents to (if it becomes a habit) failing a class or expulsion from school. **4.** something most kids do every now and then to attain feelings of freedom and living on the edge that come from being out of class while everyone else is in it.

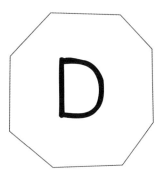

dance (n) **1.** a social function, usually with a theme. **2.** a mini version of prom, but much more casual. **3.** the cause of much anxiety, especially regarding who one will go with, or, if one goes stag, who one will dance with to those painful slow songs. **4.** an evening rife with opportunity to go off and behave a little badly out back if the bored chaperones aren't paying close enough attention. **5.** in suburban and rural schools, frequently a cornerstone of homecoming week. **6.** in rough-and-tumble public schools, an event frequently forsaken altogether because it's a common venue for fights, and it's (a) too much trouble and (b) too expensive to hire cops.

date (n) **1.** a romantic outing with a boyfriend or girlfriend that may include seeing a movie, hanging out at the mall, or going to a show. **2.** an outing, the purpose of which can be somewhat elusive, whose participants are not even sure whether they were on one or just hanging out; this ambiguity, however, can be helpful in keeping things more relaxed, because once a date is formalized it can get kind of awkward. **3.** an event that has agonizing precursors such as getting someone's digits, calling someone for the first time, and waiting for someone to call. **4.** an act that one must often work up to after days (or possibly weeks) of stressing, obsessing, and rehearsing. **5.** something boys typically feel responsible for initiating, either because of culture or genetic makeup; some boys say they like to get asked out by girls, but in general it freaks them out.

debate (n) **1.** a structured argument that usually takes place in a social studies or history class in which opposing sides must defend a position on some issue that may be ripped from a textbook (The Federalist Debate: Go!) or ripped from the headlines (Did the US government have enough evidence to declare war on Iraq? Go!). **2.** an extremely nerve-wracking and combative event in which one can be made to look like a total loser by either sitting there without saying anything or being pitted against someone who studied really hard in preparation and knows everything about his or her argument (or is kind of a show-off jerk); it doesn't help that the teacher is sitting nearby making little notations in a notebook whenever someone speaks, and that he or she explained very clearly at the beginning of the semester that class participation would account for 25 percent of the grade.

depressed, to be (n) **1.** to feel really, really, really bad. **2.** a condition not uncommon among teens; in fact, if one never, ever feels depressed in high school, there might be something wrong. **3.** if it lasts a while, a condition for which parents may send their kid to the school shrink, encourage involvement in sports (even for the un-athletic), or ask about drug use (even if you tell them that *they* are the reason for the depression in the first place). **4.** a feeling that should not persist with any consistency; those who feel this way *all* the time should probably talk to a professional about it, since there is no point going through all of high school being any more miserable than need be.

detention (n) **1.** punishment for doing things like cutting class, getting in a fight, or maybe cheating. **2.** a place one must go to after school to sit around doing nothing with a random collection of delinquents. **3.** a fairly boring experience, but not excruciating, which is why it's not much of a deterrent and the same people wind up there over and over again.

diploma (n) **1.** a piece of paper one gets upon graduation from high school. **2.** something nice to have when it is first received, but will seldom be of use thereafter (colleges will ask to see a transcript, not a diploma). **3.** a piece of paper that will take up space in one's house long after graduating from college, getting a job, and perhaps even starting a family, because no one can ever really throw out a high school diploma.

DIY (n) abbreviation for do-it-yourself. **1.** a movement espoused by members of the craft cult (and birthed by the punks) whose followers can be identified by their assorted accessories (and, in extreme cases, clothing) made of duct tape; knitting kits whipped out during free period and at lunch; ever-present copies of *ReadyMade* and *Make* magazines; and T-shirts made out of old T-shirts.

drugs (n) **1.** chemicals that high school kids put into their bodies to feel more charged, more out of it, or just more in control than they really are of anything; examples range from marijuana to cocaine to MDMA, heroin, and all kinds of prescription pills, which can be easier to get because they are either a little sister's ADHD meds or Mom's valium. **2.** illegal substances, the buying, selling, and possessing of which can land a kid in that awesome place known as juvenile court. **3.** uppers and downers that people take to feel up or down, but sometimes get addicted to and then forget what feeling naturally up or down (or even normal) is like. **4.** a prime reason one may be grounded, as parents, teachers, and substance abuse counselors are typically freaked out when they find a teenager hiding, handling, smoking, or sometimes even just thinking about drugs.

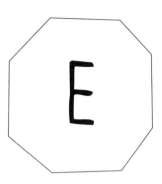

easy A (n) **1.** a class that, as long as one shows up and pays even the slightest bit of attention, is pretty much a guaranteed A (e.g., PE and health). **2.** a class for which the teacher is lazy, distracted, scared the kids will revolt, or would rather use his or her free time to work on a novel instead of grading papers. **3.** an assignment that is cake.

educational films (n) **1.** movies that aim to instruct kids about issues such as drugs and alcohol, sex, and drunk driving.

2. usually corny or dated movies that try to seem cool and talk to students on their level but fall short of even keeping them awake. **3.** movies that if actually on film (as in celluloid on spool) will break a few times during the showing. **4.** a diversion so that one can nap or flirt with a crush in class while the lights are out.

English class (n) **1.** a class focusing on the study of literature and writing. **2.** a class that offers some room for B.S.-ing, as interpretation is a cornerstone of decoding literary works; the flip side is that too much B.S.-ing, can make one want to throw up. **3.** a forum for the essay (which is much harder than math to cheat on) and poetry, which is excruciating and might as well be written in Greek or Farsi, in which case a student would have a better excuse for not understanding it whatsoever. **4.** a class that will drive math and science kids crazy, but that the drama and emo kids will probably love. **5.** an opportunity to read some good books, which (bonus!) might come up later on a reading list in college.

essay (n) **1.** expository prose presenting an argument or narrative. **2.** a type of assignment that might appear on a standardized test or as a final in English class and is particularly hard to cheat on, as it involves writing and thinking.
3. a requirement for most college applications, where it is known as the "personal essay" and one is asked to either supply a personal statement, ruminate on an influential person, or to fill a completely intimidating "blank slate" and write about *anything*, as long as it's profound, moving, insightful, and elegantly crafted.

evil teacher (n) **1.** the teacher who rules the classroom with an iron first, and has zero tolerance for talking in class, cell phones, not paying attention, and being late. **2.** a faculty member who has the ability to terrify all students, even the ones with major attitude problems, and who plays mind games with their students and employs public embarrassment as a primary tool in their reign of terror. **3.** someone who usually teaches a very hard class and has extremely high

evil teacher

standards; may be one of the best teachers you have in **high school** because you do actually learn in his or her class. **4.** a possibly very nice, approachable person in real life who just wants students to learn. **5.** a possibly mean, bitter person in real life who is taking a recent divorce out on everyone in class.

extra credit (n)

1. additional work done for the purpose of boosting one's grade. **2.** additional work done to pass a **class** needed to **graduate** (after bombing the **final exam**), or in the name of scoring the title of **valedictorian** (even though you are only a **freshman**). **3.** an assignment that can involve tasks such as (a) cooking a dish of foreign cuisine for a foreign language class, (b) reading coverage of a genocidal atrocity in *The New York Times* and writing a summary of it, or (c) helping a **teacher** put dorky posters up on the walls.

extracurricular activities (n)

1. organized stuff one participates in after school, such as sports, **clubs**, or the **school play**. **2.** activities of which some kids do an insane amount, either because they are hyped-up on **school spirit**, their **parents** make them do it, or they are trying to pack their **college application** in hopes of getting into their school of choice. **3.** in urban areas, activities that are pushed to keep kids "off the street" (though a part-time **job** is another option, and that would actually make some money).

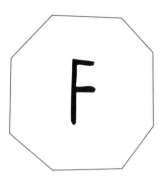

Facebook (n) **1.** a social networking site with a cleaner, more dignified design than **MySpace** but that also makes everyone's page look the same. **2.** a site with self-help quizzes and modes to brutally compare friends, engage in "poke" wars, and receive loads of wonderful criticism from anonymous posters about personality and appearance.

fail (v) **1.** to totally blow it on a test or in a **class**, earning a grade of D or, worse, F. **2.** what happens when one doesn't **study**, pay attention, or go to class very much. **3.** a bummer when the thing failed is a test, but not necessarily the end of the world, especially if it is not a frequent occurrence; a student can still pass a class

fail

after failing a test if he or she passes all of the other tests and maybe does some extra credit. **4.** a bigger bummer when the thing failed is a class, as it will definitely bring down the all-important GPA and may lead to summer school and even being held back (but hey, Einstein failed some classes, didn't he?).

fake ID (n) **1.** a form of identification used to claim that one is older than he or she really is. **2.** in high schools, a necessity to get into 18-and-over clubs before turning 18; in college, a necessity to get into bars before turning 21. **3.** the borrowed driver's license of an older sibling who may or may not look anything like the sibling borrowing it. **4.** an unconvincing counterfeit or tampered-with document (sometimes a license that has been "chalked") that bears an actual photo

of the user. **5.** a formality; bouncers always know when an ID is fake, but if the club is out to make money, they will let in just about anyone (and especially girls) anyway. **6.** a crime; tampering with federal documents or impersonating someone else is a big legal no-no and could lead to arrest, though it almost never does. **7.** the use of which is totally nerve-wracking, primarily because of number 6, but also because it just sucks to get turned down at a club; the words "Can I see your ID?" set your heart racing, though in 10 years from now, they will make you very happy. **8.** a federal offense, though it's rare that kids will get sent to jail for it.

fame (n) **1.** widespread reputation and adoration. **2.** an achievement that one may strive for by making music in a band, having a

blog, or attempting to go on TV. **3.** something that some kids in high school seem to really, really want and passionately believe will make their lives perfect. **4.** something that actually requires hard work to achieve and that hopefully (a) pays off and (b) is still desired when it comes.

fat (adj) **1.** overweight in one form or another, from chunky to obese. **2.** a description thrown around too easily by boys to describe girls who don't hold up to the anorexic, fashion magazine cover model image. **3.** a description thrown around too easily by girls to describe themselves ("Oh my God, I'm so fat!"), when often it's not the slightest bit true.

fight (n) **1.** a conflict. **2.** an hour of screaming and crying between a boyfriend and girlfriend,

a kid and his parents, or two girls arguing over the same guy. **3.** a crowd-drawing physical conflict that spontaneously erupts in the hallway and is centered around an unpredictable vortex of fists and limbs that typically, but not always, are attached to boys. **4.** a scary event that takes place at an appointed time after school, which can be more serious than an on-campus fight because the parties involved have agreed to a scheduled duel.

final exams (n) **1.** major tests at the end of each semester that make up a huge percentage of one's grade and therefore constitute (a) a lifesaver if one has slept through the semester but excels when cramming for big tests, or (b) some seriously bad news if one sucks at stressful tests and runs the risk of flushing the whole semester's work down the toilet. **2.** a fairly pointless exercise at the end of senior year if one has already been accepted to college. **3.** tests that require lots of studying, perhaps even some all-nighters, (of course, this leaves one feeling wasted and not really prepared for a big test at all). **4.** the last hurdle before the freedom of summer break.

fire drill (n) **1.** an exercise to practice evacuating the school campus should a fire/bomb scare occur; marked by an extremely loud and jarring bell that has seemingly been delivered from the depths of hell and never fails to inspire sheer panic. **2.** a procedure that requires students to trot out to the edge of school grounds then wait for all the hoopla to be over, which means that if one was in PE and wearing only shorts and now it's snowing outside, it especially sucks, or if one was making out with someone in a broom closet, he or she most likely got tossed out by a hall monitor. **3.** a godsend if one is scheduled to take a test but is not prepared, because there's a chance the test will be postponed. **4.** occasionally, an event masterminded by some kid who thought it would be funny to set the alarm off, which sometimes it is.

first day of school (n) **1.** the start of each school year. **2.** a day that many fantasize will be the unveiling of a totally brand-new version of themselves: full of self-esteem, over all that crap from last year, ready to ace all classes, and, most important, hot; the excitement lasts for about a week, until the really significant changes (the overweight kid lost a ton of weight, the geeky kid got contacts and is now actually kind of cute, a blond chick dyed her hair black) are assimilated, and then it's business as usual and everyone realizes that everyone is pretty much who they were in June. **3.** a decent opportunity to psychologically make a fresh start and, at the very least, score a lot of new clothes at Mom and Dad's expense during back-to-school shopping.

flirt (v) **1.** to engage in playful amorous behavior that may, or may not, have serious intentions. **2.** to partake in a wide variety of (sometimes counter-intuitive) activities such as: laughing at someone's jokes, making fun of someone, sitting really close to them at lunch, stealing their stuff, flattering them, arguing with them, or non-aggressively hitting them (because you really want to touch them but don't know

how). **3.** to participate in an intricate and maddening dance with another person, in which both people are trying to determine if the one likes the other, but never really find out.

football (n) **1.** a sport, often the most popular one at a school, that is played by the biggest, widest guys on campus. **2.** an activity around which whole communities rally. **3.** an obsession for students, teachers, and parents in many areas of the country. **4.** the players of which can date anyone they want (unless they are benchwarmers, but even that counts for something), often receive special treatment from teachers, and, if they're really good, will get a scholarship to college.

foreign exchange student (n) **1.** a student visiting from another country, either for a few weeks or even a year. **2.** a person who's invariably hot because of his or her sheer "otherness" and cute accent. **3.** the subject of much fascination and speculation, as well as intense battling and maneuvering to win his or her affection even though the FES likely has a really hot boyfriend or girlfriend back home or is just too shy to talk to anyone anyway.

foreign language teachers (n) **1.** frequently the most eccentric educators in the school who insist on being called "madam" or "señor." **2.** harmless but annoying teachers who plaster classrooms with posters of the Eiffel Tower and Rome's Coliseum, while also giving students extra credit for making flan, gazpacho, and spanakopita.

freshmen (n) **1.** students in their first year of high school who are extremely awkward, short, and all-around spazzy, no matter how hard they try to be cool; may still be getting a handle on the whole puberty thing. **2.** easy prey for the ridicule and bullying of sophomores, who are just psyched not to be on the bottom rung of the social ladder anymore.

friend teacher (n) **1.** an instructor who really wants to be students' friends more than their teacher. **2.** a teacher who asks students to call him or her by a first name and really should have been a college professor but doesn't have the necessary qualifications (or just couldn't get a college-level teaching job). **3.** an educator who can't give up the idea that they are no longer young. **4.** a teacher whose classroom is decorated with

fund-raising

posters of under-appreciated indie bands and obscure luminaries in their field. **5.** in some cases, one's favorite teacher because he or she sees each student as a full person, not just another statistic.

fund-raising (v) **1.** the selling of all kinds of crap in order to subsidize a school activity or group, such as a class trip or the cheerleading squad. **2.** carrying around a box of overpriced candy or a catalog for wrapping paper and begging people to buy stuff they don't need. **3.** in some cases, going door to door in one's neighborhood, holding a car wash, or, if one gets desperate, putting up a lemonade stand. **4.** asking parents to ask/force their friends and coworkers to fork over some money or, if they can't be bothered to do that, just write a check themselves for that whole box of candy and eat it or throw it away.

gay (adj) **1.** homosexual; to be into people of one's own gender in a romantic / sexual way. **2.** amazingly enough, still seen as a stigma in lots of schools, though it's a lot more acceptable today than it was a few years ago. **3.** a description for the really sensitive boys in high school who girls think would make great boyfriends … if they didn't already have boyfriends themselves. **4.** *slang:* stupid or dumb ("That chem lab was so gay."); this usage is used by people who (a) have no idea what "gay" really means, (b) don't see that it is offensive to gay people to call dumb things "gay," or (c) don't care if it is offensive because they are real jerks.

girlfriend (n) See boy-friend / girlfriend.

girls (n) **1.** people possessing certain biological equipment. **2.** the gender that likes to communicate quite frequently through texting, talking, writing notes, and however else they can. **3.** a complete mystery to boys, who pretend to know what girls are talking about even when they don't have a clue and are really just trying hard not to look at their **breasts**. **4.** the gender that tends to smell better and cares, in general, more about **clothes** and fashion.

gossip (n) **1.** hearsay about one's fellow classmates that spreads like wildfire, frequently getting wildly distorted in the process. **2.** dirt on someone who has no idea that dirt is being spread around about them. **3.** an amusing thing when it's not about you, and a potentially life-destroying thing when it is. **4.** something that is passed on, particularly by great storytellers who are also insecure and know that gossiping is a great way to get attention. **5.** talk that for some unknown reason is deemed true even with no proof and, even with insane amounts of certified evidence, is almost impossible to get disproved (once spoken, everyone will believe it really happened in some form or another forever). **6.** a precursor to the **rumor**, which should be regarded with the utmost skepticism, as rumors tend to be based on little truth and are usually attached to a personal motive of the spreader.

gossip

goth

goth (n) **1.** kids who wear all black, dye their hair black, wear chains, and use heavy black makeup. **2.** those who identify strongly with the music they listen to, which is usually stuff like SlipKnot, Rammstien, A.F.I., and Korn. **3.** an angry or depressed person who is having a hell of a hard time in high school, or an upbeat, nice person whose dark style feels (to others) completely incongruent with his or her true personality.

GPA (n) abbreviation for grade point average. **1.** the weighted, numerical summation of a student's efforts from semester to semester. **2.** something that can be totally screwed up by one impossible AP physics class, or the semester that you actually had a boyfriend or girlfriend. **3.** like an SAT score, a highly reductive number that greatly influences the quality of a college application. **4.** a number that determines who will be valedictorian and who will be repeating senior year (see super senior).

graduation

graduation (n) **1.** the culminating event of high school. **2.** a ceremony that involves wearing extremely cheap, overpriced polyester caps and gowns in school colors, and having a picture (which a graduate's parents can buy for the low, low price of $19.95) taken the instant someone, such as the principal, hands over one's diploma. **3.** a kind of big deal, if only because it means figuring out what to do with one's life.

graffiti (n) **1.** images and words left on public surfaces using mostly markers and spray paint and considered art by some and vandalism by others. **2.** scrawl covering school bathroom walls that (a) consists of both valuable information and outright lies about one's classmates and (b) often comes to serve as an old friend while sitting on the bowl and gazing at it every day. **3.** a practice, also known as tagging, used mainly by gang members to identify turf around the school and city. **4.** stuff scrawled on a bus' posters and seats or scratched into its windows quickly so that the driver does not see. **5.** totally uninspired doodles and drivel scribbled onto a desk or perhaps the chair directly in front of a seat (someone's name, a gash carved with a ballpoint pen, a solo tic-tac-toe game, or something completely stupid like "My balls were here").

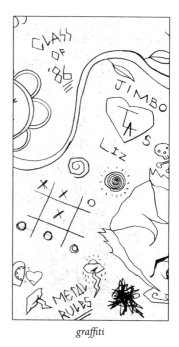

graffiti

grounded, **to be** (v)
1. to endure some form of punishment that's been established by one's **parents** for what they consider wrongdoing, such as missing **curfew**, **cutting class**, or being found in a half-clothed state with a **boyfriend** or **girlfriend**. **2.** to suffer a decided upon term of hardship that varies in length depending on one's parents and the crime in question and most likely includes the prohibition of seeing a boyfriend or girlfriend (or any friends at all for that matter), using a **cell phone**, enjoying any online, TV, or driving activities, or (for really bad crimes) attending the **prom** or **class trip**.

group project (n) **1.** an academic exercise that requires several people to work cooperatively. **2.** a real pain because in any group there's going to be someone

really irritating, someone who is ridiculously lazy, and someone who is an anal perfectionist. **3.** an opportunity to socialize without getting grief from **parents** ("I have to stay late at Whoever's house to work on the group project"); also an opportunity to stay late at Whoever's house without working on the group project at all.

guidance counselor (n)
1. a **high school** administrator who helps students pick **classes** and research **colleges**. **2.** an overworked school staff member who is supposed to provide guidance but has so many students to attend to that he or she doesn't really know who any of those students are. **3.** the staff person with the cushiest office, which has posters of idyllic-looking college campuses (i.e., marketing materials from the schools) all over the walls. **4.** in some cases,

a favorite staff member because he or she is interested in students' futures and doesn't dole out grades.

reality hits—unless they take three gym classes the final semester of **senior** year, they won't **graduate**.

guys (n) See **boys**.

gym (n) **1.** scheduled physical activity at school. **2.** a forced, inane **class** that sometimes involves wearing unflattering garments that look like they were made in Russia 50 years ago and may require getting undressed and/or showering in a room with people one doesn't know or like. **3.** the most annoying class for **girls** who have their **period**, especially when the activity is swimming. **4.** a forum for social humiliation through the forever painful activity of picking teams. **5.** a class everyone thinks they can **cut** (it's gym! who cares!?) until

haircut (n) **1.** an alteration in the length or look of one's hair. **2.** a potential complete disaster that is sure to elicit crying. **3.** an evolution in personal style so grand that it is on par with the overthrow of an old political regime and the installation of a new one, e.g., the hippie girl who had long hair forever and is now sporting a pixie cut and hanging out with guys in bands, and the Goody Two-Shoes blond guy who went emo over the summer and now has jet-black hair.

hallway (n) **1.** neutral space in the corridors of a high school building. **2.** a potential danger zone (if a fight breaks out) that at certain times requires permission to walk down, which comes in the form of a hall pass. **3.** a bad place to be if one is cutting class and hall monitors or teachers are doing a hallway "sweep."

hanging out (n) **1.** a generic term used to refer to just about anything one does alone or in a group outside of school: watching movies, going to the mall, playing video games, chatting online, listening to music, shopping, staring off into space. **2.** a code word for "making out with my boyfriend/girlfriend in his/her bedroom when no parents were at home."

held back (v) **1.** not advancing to the next grade. **2.** what happens when a student cuts every class for the whole year, fails all tests, and/or gets mono or something equally bad. **3.** a painful result of either bad decisions or bad luck, especially because one then has to take classes with annoying younger people (though that can also open the dating pool). **4.** an avoidable consequence if a student endures summer school.

high school (n.) **1.** after middle school, the place one goes to learn the basics in a variety of subjects in hopes of becoming a person with some kind of clue about how things work. **2.** a purgatory of sorts that one must endure (and graduate from) in order to enter college or the workplace. **3.** a four-year rite of passage between the preteen years and adulthood that offers up a detailed education in social politics, identity formation, sex, drugs, and melodrama. **4.** one of the most formative and unifying aspects of US culture (pretty much everyone goes because it is the law).

hip-hop kids (n) **1.** kids who adopt the fashion, speech patterns, slang, and music of the hip-hop genre. **2.** kids who have the amazing ability to spontaneously craft poetic and/or rhyming verse, which they may use to slyly poke fun at people or offer cutting social commentary; either talent or marketing genius may

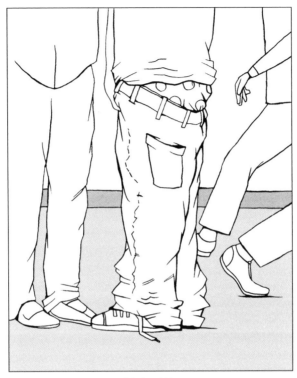

hip-hop kids

make them millionaires and/or franchise creators someday. **3.** walking billboards for a multimillionaire rap mogul, or someone who actually thinks wearing pants halfway down one's butt looks good. **4.** rich, white, suburban kids who adopt a ghetto pose, even though they live in a tree-lined cul-de-sac.

homecoming (n) **1.** a tradition that takes place in the fall that lasts as long as a week. **2.** an orgy of school spirit that typically involves a big game (usually football) played on the home field, a dance (kind of like a fall prom), and other assorted activities like a pep rally and themed dress-up days. **3.** a throwback to the era of sock hops, glee clubs, and going steady; popular in the Midwest where there's not a whole lot else going on.

homeroom (n) **1.** the class students report to every morning where attendance is taken. **2.** a room with a random collection of students attempting to wake up and do the homework they blew off the night before. **3.** where to meet up with boyfriends, girlfriends, or best friends every day to make plans for lunch or plot what class you might cut together.

homework (n) **1.** academic exercises such as reading, writing essays, and doing math problems. **2.** something that one is supposed to do at home but that usually gets done on the school bus, in homeroom, or in the cafeteria. **3.** arguably one of the most irritating aspects of high school since the whole point of *going* to school is to work *there* and not at home.

hook up (v) **1.** to engage in intimate physical activities with someone else, the parameters of which are a little vague but generally mean at least making out. **2.** an expression frequently used in the third person past tense to relay a piece of gossip, i.e. "Eli and Carolyn hooked up last night." **3.** the vague way of telling friends what went down between

hot teacher

oneself and a **guy** or **girl** at a **party** ("So, what happened?" "We 'hooked up.'")

hot teacher (n) **1.** that rare educator who is an authority figure, determines students' grades, and is, um, sexy. **2.** a distracting male or female, usually on the young side, who has amazingly well-behaved classrooms; most likely candidates are **English teachers**. **3.** when female, a teacher with perky **breasts** and pretty hair; when male, a teacher with boyish good looks and a slightly geeky demeanor undercut by a *Dead Poet's Society* fashion sense and a **cool** briefcase.

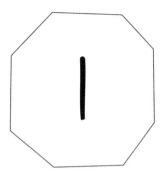

IB classes (n) abbreviation for International Baccalaureate classes. **1.** hard classes that smart and ambitious kids take to earn the IB diploma, which looks very good on a college application; subjects range from biology to film to art history. **2.** an alternative to AP classes; both can potentially get you college credit, but IB classes also have an international focus. **3.** courses that require completing something called an "internal assessment," which sounds like a grueling doctor's appointment but is actually a very long paper that is written throughout the semester on a topic that usually is not covered in class and has little relevance to one's life at all.

ID (n) **1.** a card or piece of paper that affirms your identity. **2.** the thing no one ever wants to lose because it's a real pain in the butt to replace. **3.** the worst picture anyone will ever mug for, regardless of what year it's taken. **4.** the thing teens attempt to tamper with when they want to get in somewhere that they're not old enough to get into (see fake ID).

insecurity (n) **1.** self-doubt, lack of confidence, or, as parents and teachers would say, "low self-esteem." **2.** one of the cornerstones of the high school experience, which everyone — yes, everyone — feels. **3.** the primary emotion that leads to one becoming a bitch, a jerk, a slut, or a copycat, or to gossiping, making fun of people, doing drugs, being in a clique, lying, being a straight-A student, wearing expensive clothes, and just about everything that goes on in high school (which is all about not knowing who one is yet). *antonym:* self-esteem.

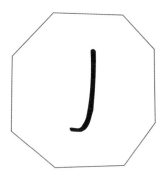

janitors (n) **1.** people who clean the school. **2.** people worthy of sympathy, because they have to clean up stuff like moldy food from lockers and who-knows-what from the bathrooms. **3.** the ones who collect all of the recycling from the various classrooms and thus have total access to private notes that contain the secrets of one's social life (assuming they are even interested).

jerk (n) **1.** an unnecessarily mean, brutish, typically thick-necked guy, who is cruel to people just because. **2.** a popular but also insecure jock or really "cool" guy who seeks to boost his own status by belittling others. **3.** a purveyor of gossip and generator of rumors or out-right lies. **4.** a big flirt who leads girls on, gets them to do things they are not sure they should be doing, and then does not call them again. **5.** the male version of the bitch, who he may in fact date. **6.** you, when you're having a bad day.

job (n) **1.** a thing one does for money. **2.** a gig that often involves wearing a hideous outfit and taking orders from a person one may not like very much. **3.** a task friends make fun of, until they need to borrow some money. **4.** a great way to make parents think one is responsible, as well as to earn money to buy a car, blow on video games and movies, and pay for dates.

jock (n) **1.** a guy or girl who is really into sports, playing one almost every season; may be a member of varsity. **2.** a student who may get preferential treatment in a class if the teacher is a big sports fan and knows that the student *must* pass in order to stay on the team and help win the big game. **3.** in some cases, a bit of a player *off* the field who is double-timing it with several cheerleaders.

juniors (n) **1.** third-year students. **2.** in all likelihood, the most stressed-out people on campus because the third year of high school matters most on an academic record—plus it's the time when students are preparing to apply for college, taking a ton of standardized tests, working part-time jobs, and trying to have a life.

I-J

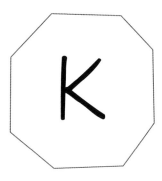

keg (n) **1.** a giant container of beer found at house parties. **2.** a gift from an older sibling, seeing as it is nearly impossible (and totally illegal) for a high school student to obtain a keg on his or her own. **3.** a sure sign a party will get out of control, likely ending with lots of people hooking up, fights breaking out, someone crying, valuable items getting broken, and someone getting grounded.

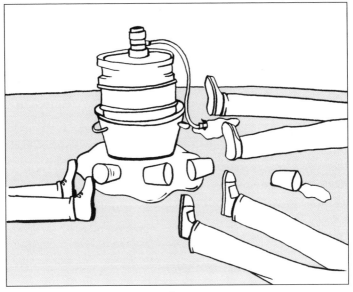

keg

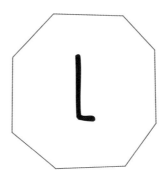

label (n) **1.** a classification (goth, punk, nerd, jock) that puts people into categories, and by which they can be easily judged negatively or positively, though more frequently the former. **2.** a way to reduce people to neat stereotypes, enabling one to dismiss any of the more complex nuances that invariably make up the target's identity and personality. **3.** a grouping people sometimes use for themselves (i.e., "I am a total geek") so as to establish an identity or articulate what music they

like, who they hang out with, and what activities they partake in.

library (n) **1.** a space filled with books and other reference materials to aid one in research. **2.** a place where one goes to study, though eating, flirting, and sleeping inevitably also take place here. **3.** a fine place to kill time during a free period, but hanging out with friends can be difficult here, as librarians will not tolerate any breaking of their code of silence (note: if one does fall out of their good graces, said librarians can often be charmed with an earnest inquiry regarding reference materials on an obscure topic).

lie (n) **1.** a false statement. **2.** an invitation to get busted. **3.** an untruth that can range from a small white lie, such as saying that one is studying at a friend's house when one is really headed to the movies, to a major whopper of a lie, like cheating on the SAT or professing one's fidelity to a boyfriend or girlfriend when one has been totally unfaithful. **4.** the telling of which can create a habit (known as "lying"), which brings with it a number of unhappy side effects, including guilt and a constant feeling of dread that you will not be able to keep all of your stories straight. **5.** a thing you are either good at telling (some kids are great liars, and never get caught)

or not good at telling (people think you are lying even when you are, in fact, telling the truth).

locker (n) **1.** a repository for all of one's crap. **2.** the place one keeps the textbook thought to be lost, rank sneakers, house keys, a busted backpack, and a Tupperware container with a three-month-old rotting lunch. **3.** a place for broadcasting one's personal identity by posting photos of a boyfriend/girlfriend, a pic of some hot celeb, Ivy League school stickers (for the offspring of particularly intense parents), high school team spirit signifiers, and announcements of political leanings ("Vote for Pedro") or jadedness ("Down With the Man"). **4.** a house for a mirror and lots of magnetic crap because everyone needs to look good and all that magnetic crap is so cheap

K-L

locker

and fun. **5.** the thing one can never open at those really important moments because one has again forgotten the combination.

loser (n) **1.** a social outcast. **2.** what everyone is afraid of being but, at times, feels like they are. **3.** what one feels like when: sitting alone at lunch, rejected by a guy/girl, or yelled at by a teacher or parent in front of friends. **4.** the guy or girl who thinks it's OK to cheat, lie, or simply be mean. **5.** one of the worst things to be called because while other insults are specific (i.e., fat, ugly, stupid), *loser* refers generally to every aspect of one's personality and being.

love (n) **1.** an overwhelming, intense feeling of affection for and devotion to a person. **2.** a sure sign that one is not thinking clearly. **3.** an emotion that is sometimes mistaken for lust or attachment (particularly if one has just had sex for the first time). **4.** a thing that some people seem to "fall in" all the time, which can become a bit tiresome for their friends.

lunch (n) **1.** a period reserved for eating. **2.** a midday break from class that shines like a beacon of freedom by mid-morning. **3.** a meal usually consumed in the cafeteria, which is ground zero for high school politics, gossip, and clique gathering. **4.** something that some students seem to have all day long ("Aren't you supposed to be in class now?" "No, I have lunch.").

K–L

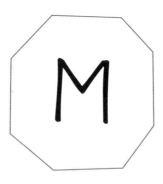

making out (v) **1.** kissing and mild groping in the corner of a room or on the corner of a street or in a backseat, or anywhere really. **2.** one of the best things about **high school**, with the right person, of course. **3.** an act that, when done with a **crush** or someone hot or really **cool**, generates a feeling that pretty much nothing else can rival. *See also* **bases** and **hooking up**.

makeup (n) **1.** cosmetics applied to a **girl's** face with the goal of improving her appearance but, when over-applied (18 layers of base, foundation, concealer, eye shadow, mascara, lipstick, and lip gloss), do exactly the opposite. **2.** something also worn by some **boys**, such as **goths**, **punks**, and emos, or simply those inspired by some guy in a **band** on **MTV**.

mall (n) **1.** an emporium of retail madness that houses **movie** theaters, **clothing** stores, and multiple places to socialize, such as the food court. **2.** a place to scope out **guys** and **girls**.

mascot

3. a popular teen hangout on Friday or Saturday nights because (a) one does not need an ID to get in and (b) it is sanitized and well-lit enough that parents feel OK about letting their kid go there.

mascot (n) **l.** a character that represents a school and frequently takes the form of an animal (cougar, tiger, hawk), but can also have more complicated and controversial forms such as the Indians. **2.** a symbol of school spirit that appears on assorted items such as T-shirts, jackets, buttons, and bumper stickers. **3.** a role a student volunteers to play, which requires donning a very hot and uncomfortable costume at games and/or **homecoming** and attempting to pump up the crowd.

math (n) short for mathematics **1.** the study of numbers, quantities, measurements, and stuff like that. **2.** **class** taken every year in a new and unfamiliar form each time (i.e., algebra, geometry, and the baddest mofo of them all—calculus), so by the time one has come close to mastering one form, it's time to take another. **3.** a real annoyance for right-brain people, who tend to do better in **English class**. **4.** a class that has 90 percent of its students asking "When am I ever going to use this in real life?" (the other 10 percent go on to study mathematics at Harvard or Yale).

movies, the (n) **1.** the cinema; a place to watch new films. **2.** the most innocuous way to get out of the house and away from **parents** for a few hours with no questions asked. **3.** where one goes to see a lot of totally stupid things on screen, which doesn't matter because the point is not enrichment, but, as discussed, getting out of the house. **4.** a hot spot for **flirting**, **hanging out**, and **making out**. **5.** a universal first or second **date** choice, especially horror films which **boys** appreciate for their gross factor and **girls** like because it gives them the opportunity to cuddle up to boys in faux (or perhaps real) fear.

MTV (n) **1.** a cable channel that once played a lot of revolutionary music videos and now plays a lot of reality shows about the same spoiled rich kids over and over. **2.** a wonder of generations past that has been replaced by the Internet, where everyone can see whatever video they want whenever they want.

music (n) **1.** songs by singers, groups, recording artists, and other music makers. **2.** medium for identifying oneself, from how cool one is to inclusion in a particular clique, whether it's hip-hop, punk, goth, or emo. **3.** a significant source of solace and pleasure, especially while dealing with a breakup, a crush, anger, or depression (so pretty much all the time). **4.** a rhythmic distraction that is particularly gratifying when played loud, either through home speakers, iPod headphones, or the stereo of a car (all the better if the car is a convertible or a van/SUV.) **5.** something that, unlike trigonometry, a person will always remember.

music

MySpace (n) **1.** a social networking site. **2.** a clunky collage of ugly and annoying neon banners, flash games, and quirky animations that people use to personalize their pages. **3.** a magnet for spam and pervs. **4.** a site in which everyone has some random welcome guy named Tom listed as "a friend." *See also* Facebook.

nerd (n) **1.** a somewhat awkward person who **studies** a lot. **2.** a threat to the easy-to-sway security of some popular people who feel that being seen talking to or even standing within 50 feet of one will disastrously affect their social status. **3.** a social outcast who finds kindred spirits with which to form an anti-**cool** gang. **4.** a **smart** kid with much greater chances of going to an Ivy League school than most of his or her peers. **5.** a technology freak, who is in the A.V. Club, hangs around the computer lab all day, hacks websites, and writes code that may (or may not) get him or her a scholarship to MIT.

nerds

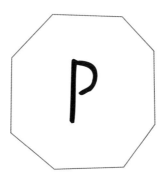

parents (n) **1.** adults who through either the act of, ahem, intimate coupling, adoption, or re-marriage have become the people who basically control one's life. **2.** the adults one can thank for clothes and food on the table and pretty much everything that makes life bearable (the TV, computers, cell phones, the car). **3.** people who tell their offspring not to do and say things they consistently do and say (perhaps because they want their kids' lives to be better or easier than theirs). **4.** people who after either seeing a Public Service Announcement about drugs, reading a worrisome article about teen sex in *Newsweek*, or hearing about a violent incident at a local high school on the news attempt to discuss these topics with their kids, resulting in awkward and questionably useful discussions.

party (n) **1.** a get-together of friends in celebration of something (like graduation) or nothing at all. **2.** a massive booze-fueled gathering sometimes also referred to as a "house party" and typically held at the home of someone whose parents have gone out of town for the weekend. **3.** an unsupervised event at which people will get wasted, make out, smoke, fight, and break stuff they shouldn't. **4.** the reason the cops are in front of one's house.

PA system (n) abbreviation for public address system. **1.** a source of announcements made during homeroom by irritatingly chipper teachers or students selected to deliver daily news; they may even try to be funny, which just makes things worse.

peer pressure (n) **1.** an exaggerated force that parents, teachers, the media, and others feel is responsible for making teenagers do things they would never ordinarily do. **2.** a phenomenon illustrated in silly and oversimplified educational films and Public Service Announcements through scenarios that depict a bunch of over-bearing "cool" people hanging out at a "crazy" party and pressuring a mindless individual into doing drugs, drinking alcohol, or having sex. **3.** a reason parents like to use to explain why their kid is acting like an idiot. **4.** something that does exist but generally manifests itself only: (a) in kids who have yet to learn how to think for themselves and (b) over long periods of time (not at just one "crazy" party), in which case it is more like *peer influence* than peer pressure.

period, class (n) **1.** the sections of a school day, each one beginning and ending with the sound of a bell. **2.** a neutral concept when spoken of in general ("I will see you after 6th period"), but one that may

P

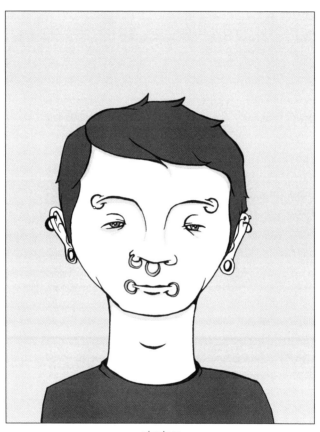

piercings

also inspire feelings of panic or dread when it's associated with a **class** one hates ("I have PE 6th period").

period, monthly (n)
1. a super fun time of the month for **girls** that comes complete with painful cramping, annoying **acne**, and a deep fear of wearing white pants or skirts. **2.** a mysterious natural phenomenon that grosses out **boys**. **3.** an excuse girls sometimes use to get out of **class** (sometimes there is truth behind it; sometimes it's a **lie**, but who is going to check?).

piercings (n) **1.** metal adornments punched through any number of body parts, including the ear, belly button, nose, eyebrow, tongue, and back of neck. **2.** something that will definitely get a rise out of **parents** who, if said piercing is on the face, will even ask one to take it out when visiting relatives (generally, the response is no). **3.** body decorations whose attractiveness is debatable and subject to personal taste and that often become less attractive over time, even to the person who once paid to have it done. **4.** something that is usually illegal for minors, though pretty much everyone knows how to get around that if they really want to.

player (n) **1.** a **guy** who gets tons of action with chicks; the number of **girls** he hasn't **hooked up** with is much smaller than the number of those he has. **2.** someone who is (a) looked up to or resented by guys with less fortunate standing, (b) looked down upon by the older, **smarter** girls who have seen their share of players and don't find them alluring, and

P

(c) sought after by everyone else. **3.** typically a seasoned senior, though in some rare impressive cases, a skillful freshman. **4.** in some ways, a male version of the slut (who, due to an incredibly unfair double standard, is actually disrespected for engaging in precisely the same behavior).

pledge of allegiance (n)
1. an antiquated oath, swearing loyalty to the United States flag and the "republic for which it stands," that many students around the country still recite every morning in homeroom. **2.** a completely rote exercise typified by the sound of completely uninspired mumbling and groaning. **3.** a somewhat controversial sing-along as there is always one radical or atheist kid who makes a political issue of the pledge and refuses to stand until (a) our government stops "oppressing and

terrorizing its own citizens" or (b) the word "God" is taken out of the pledge; this kid and the one radical or religious kid who thinks prayer should be mandatory in public school are generally not friends.

poetry (n) **1.** an inscrutable form of literature studied in English class. **2.** something one is constantly asked to interpret which comes easily for kids who are highly introspective or good at B.S.-ing and is the bane of existence for the rest of the class. **3.** painfully awkward or just plain bad writing of deeply sensitive emo or depressed kids, who post it on their blogs for the world to see. **4.** a dating asset: guys who actually get poetry can use it to woo pretty girls.

pop quiz (n) **1.** a surprise short test. **2.** an easy A for anyone who's been listening at all or doing some of the required reading. **3.** an evil, guerilla tactic executed by teachers who are either feeling too lazy to teach, or have really had it with no one paying attention in class and want to bust everyone who's been slacking.

principal (n) **1.** the big cheese at school who opens assemblies, walks the halls, and waits for students to get in trouble. **2.** the person who works in the "principal's office," a place one gets sent to when one has really messed up and where that student's parents are invited to discuss the infraction.

private school (n) **1.** an educational facility that one must gain admission to and that one's parents must pay thousands and thousands of dollars for the privilege of sending their kid there. **2.** a learning environment that is way less likely than a

private school kid

P

public school to have police roaming the campus or metal detectors set up at the entrance. **3.** despite what parents think, a prime location for things like sex, booze, and drugs (even more so than most public schools because private school kids typically have more money to throw around).

prom

prom (n) **1.** a formal dance extravaganza at the end of the school year that causes much freaking out. **2.** an excuse to ask out a **crush**, or at least to come up with some even better excuse not to. **3.** a perfectly good reason to hate people with **boyfriends** and **girlfriends** who do not have to worry about finding a **date** or enduring the indignity of wondering if someone will go with them, if someone is out of their league, if someone would give a look of incredulity and confusion upon being asked, or if someone will ask them to go simply because someone else said no. **4.** an event that inspires even normal **girls** to obsess over finding the perfect attire and ask their **parents** to spend an obscene amount of money on not only the frock, but also a wide array of accessories, which can range from very sparkly jewelry to teeny-tiny coordinating purses to, uh, tiaras. **5.** the one time that a teenage **guy** will agree to wear a tux, generally because he knows that if he does, the odds of getting some action are much better. **6.** an event that comes with a lesson (sometimes unsuccessful) in how to attach a horrid flower to a girl's dress without pricking her in the boob. **7.** an opportunity for a lame photographer to take some photos that will later document, no matter how **cool** one is, how big of a dork everyone was, and how that "perfect" outfit was actually not so hot. **8.** an event during which one is expected to partake in illicit drinking, stay out past **curfew**, and lose one's virginity, even if (a) one really doesn't want to, (b) it has already been lost, or (c) one goes with a friend.

P

PSATs (n) **1.** a test, typically taken in sophomore year, that provides a preview as to how one is going to do on the SATs.

PTA (n) abbreviation for Parents and Teachers Association. **1.** parents and school administrators who meet regularly to hear parents complain about stuff they think sucks about the school. **2.** an organization that holds bake sales, at which they hock cupcakes, lemonade, and baggies of chocolate chip cookies—which range from really good to burnt and disgusting—outside the auditorium during the school play and at other schoolwide functions.

public school (n) **1.** an educational facility funded by tax dollars (teachers' salaries, books, electricity). **2.** a school where any kid who lives nearby can go for free; often rougher than a private school, but also more reflective of the real world in terms of socio-economic makeup. **3.** in big cities, a madhouse bursting with thousands of students where fights break out daily and cops are occasionally on the scene. **4.** in wealthy suburbs, a school that may as well be private since one has to be rich to live there (i.e., be in that school district).

punk (n) **1.** a kid who has adopted the fashion sense of the punk movement of London in the 1970s (wearing things like leather jewelry adorned with spikes, anything ripped, tight jeans, assorted chains, the use of safety pins in various ways, and, in some cases, a mohawk) and often is a fan of music like the Dead Kennedys and the Sex Pistols. **2.** a pro-anarchy youth who is all about political and social revolt; sometimes it's because he or she believes in a cause (vegetarianism, legalizing marijuana), and sometimes it's simply for the sake of revolting.

purse (n) **1.** a satchel girls use to carry stuff around, most of it having nothing to do with school. **2.** a repository for makeup, a mirror, a cell phone, gum, ID, writing utensils, and maybe cigarettes. **3.** in some wealthy schools, a major status symbol, with the latest Prada, Fendi, and Louis Vuitton bags making their debut on the first day of school.

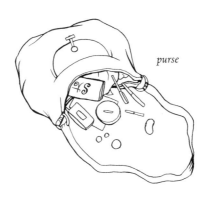

purse

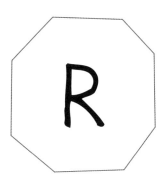

reach school (n)
1. a college or university to which one applies but has no chance in hell of getting in.

relationship (n)
1. a committed partnership between two people that usually comes about after a few dates or time spent hanging out. **2.** a reason to get up and go to school every day. **3.** a source of gloating, giddiness, and sometimes sheer stupidity. **4.** a string of unmet expectations, fights, and maybe even infidelities, which therefore eventually ends with a breakup. **5.** an effort (usually on the part of the boys) to get regular action. **6.** a time-consuming and, oftentimes, expensive endeavor that is generally worth the trouble if one can learn something from it.

rumor (n) **1.** a juicy bit of information that gets spread like wildfire, even though most people who utter it have no idea how true (or not) it is. **2.** endless fodder for cafeteria downtime and bathroom gossip. **3.** a lie that often includes ridiculous and obviously untrue content.

R

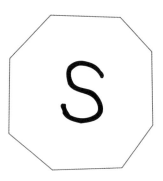

SAT (n) **1.** a test that was named and renamed the Scholastic Aptitude Test, Scholastic Assessment Test, and Scholastic Achievement Test, but since various people always felt it was mislabeled, now officially stands for … nothing.
2. a long, scary test that determines, in large part, where one will go to college.
3. a standardized test for which one learns words one may never utter again, and mathematic principles one was probably already taught but can't remember.
4. a stalwart of the college application process that has come under fire for being biased and not necessarily a clear indicator of future academic success. **5.** a test easier for kids with parents who are willing to mortgage the house in order to pay for private SAT prep classes, which may or may not help.

safety school (n) **1.** the college or university that a student pretty much knows he or she is getting into and, in fact, will go to if not accepted anywhere else.

scholarship (n) **1.** free money for college! sweet! **2.** a financial award one receives for being super smart, super broke, a standout sports jock, or a minority (amazingly, at application time, everyone is suddenly one-eighth Native American) or for having an amazing skill (fencing, viola, underwater basket weaving). **3.** something that, despite all of the categories listed in number 2, is difficult to obtain because everyone wants free money for college.

school newspaper (n) **1.** a school publication written by and for students. **2.** a small-time news rag that can be good but is frequently lame and taken way too seriously by its contributors because at age 16 they've already decided they're going to work for *The New York Times* and win a Pulitzer. **3.** a great addition to a college application. **4.** a tool of self-expression that students will sometimes use to print something controversial, eventually getting administrators and outraged parents involved; this pretty much only serves to remind people that the school has a newspaper in the first place.

school play (n) **1.** a theatrical production, usually put on twice a year. **2.** a source of much stress among those who are in it and/or want to be in it. **3.** an ordeal that involves the painful process of auditions, and the excruciating part of casting announcements, through which one often learns they did not get the part they wanted. **4.** an endeavor seen by some participants as *ohmygodthemostimportantthingever*, which can be kind of annoying. **5.** a total time suck that requires many, many hours

school spirit

of rehearsal, during which cast members become **best friends** (until the play is over). **6.** a magnet for overly expressive, loud, and actor-y types who are hard to take in large doses.

school shrink (n) **1.** a mental health professional who works on campus about two days a week. **2.** the person a student gets sent to talk to about any genuine troubles, depression, eating disorders, or instances of "acting out." **3.** generally a nice, but not always effective, person who spends a lot of time trying to get teens to "open up"; may recommend that a student sees a bona fide outside shrink if he or she thinks that the student is troubled, **depressed**, angry, or skinny enough to warrant it.

school spirit (n) **1.** enthusiasm about one's school and its sports teams. **2.** school pride exhibited through the wearing of logo-emblazoned **clothing** such as T-shirts and jackets, and rooting hard core at games, especially during **homecoming**. **3.** for some, a great uniting force, especially if a school's sports team is pretty good. **4.** for others, a completely ridiculous idea.

S-T

science fair (n) **1.** a competition pitting projects that demonstrate scientific principles or research. **2.** a chance for non-jocks to participate in some kind of competitive activity that generally involves totally unoriginal projects like bubbling volcanoes and evaporation exhibits. **3.** a gateway event to the Siemens Competition in Math, Science and Technology, the World Series of science fairs for which students and teachers will commit hundreds of hours to projects that include things like inventing a jet pack, curing cancer, and creating a sustainable alternative to gasoline out of root beer or bubble wrap.

secondary sex characteristics (n) **1.** changes to one's body that start to occur at puberty and really pick up steam in high school (i.e., the growth of breasts and hair — armpit, facial, and pubic — and the onset of periods). **2.** bodily developments that are not so exciting when one sees them taking place in one's own body, but annoyingly exciting for everyone else watching. **3.** potential popularity builders, especially during freshman and sophomore years, but by junior and senior years, everyone is pretty much on the same page and it's all a lot less novel.

secret (n) **1.** confidential information that is shared with someone with the stern, expressed condition that it not be repeated to anyone else. **2.** a story or detail that is often passed on as soon as the person who told it is out of earshot. **3.** a possible seed for gossip or a rumor.

seeing a teacher outside of school (n)
1. a totally weird and un-comfortable experience.
2. an encounter that is made weirder and more uncomfortable if the teacher is trying to dress cool (but not succeeding) or on a date with a significant other whom he or she presumably has sex with. **3.** a sighting that might be fodder for gossip or a rumor (the hot quotient of the sig-nificant other mentioned in number 2 could definitely come into play).

self-esteem (n) **1.** con-fidence in oneself. **2.** an amorphous characteristic that adults and parents say is the key to being well-adjusted, excelling in life, and resisting peer pressure. **3.** a difficult thing to *really* have in high school when constantly faced with comparisons (by oneself or others) to all the smartest,

hottest, and most creative kids on campus. **4.** a lofty goal in high school (if you feel OK about yourself from day to day, you're doing pretty good).
antonym: insecurity.

senior (n) **1.** students in their last year of high school. **2.** students who typically suffer from a condition known as senioritis and act cooler than everyone else because they've been doing the high school thing for almost four years, are bigger than every-one else, and have more developed secondary sex characteristics. **3.** kids who are both secretly freaked out about college and also excited as hell to be getting out.

senior picture (n) **1.** an obligatory, and usually retouched, portrait of a graduating student. **2.** next to a student ID, probably

S–T

the worst picture one has of oneself, either because one somehow came out looking like a dork or went over the top and tried to look all glam like a model in a cover shoot. **3.** a perfect component of a time capsule that one can bury now, dig up in as few as 10 years, and have a very long laugh.

senioritis (n) **1.** the apathy that takes over **seniors** in their last semester of **high school**, due to the fact that they're basically out of there. **2.** a condition the symptoms of which include **cutting class**, going to lots of **parties**, opting for several free **periods**, and spending a lot of time just **hanging out**.

senior picture

94

sex (n) **1.** the act of two people having intercourse. **2.** a subject that gets everyone all excited: teenagers, because many of them think about it a lot, want it, are having it, and/or think they should be having it, and parents, who worry (with some sense, actually) that their teenagers will get pregnant, contract diseases, or get "emotionally scarred" by having sex too soon. **3.** an act that is typically a bit scary the first time it is undertaken because, no matter how much preparation or thought goes into it, it is still weird and kind of awkward. **4.** something that girls (and, less frequently, guys) sometimes feel pressured into by either their romantic partners or their friends. **5.** a topic that 99 percent of the time is extraordinarily uncomfortable to speak to one's parents about; still, any advice they give about taking precautions and being responsible is usually good advice. **6.** something that guys are notorious for lying about, whether it's because they are in competition with each other, make up stories in the form of wishful thinking, or just think that they are supposed to lie about it because that's what other guys do. **7.** something no one is "supposed to" graduate from high school without having done because of some strange societally induced fear ("I don't want to go to college a virgin!"), but in reality lots of people don't have sex until college or beyond, and it really doesn't matter in the grand scheme of things. *See also* bases and sex ed.

sex ed (n) **1.** a class that teaches the nitty-gritty about sex. **2.** a painfully uncomfortable class that covers all the "ins and outs"

S-T

sick day

of sexual relations, how girls' and guys' bodies differ "down there," and the many freakish diseases one can get by having unprotected sex. **3.** a class that may be big on scare tactics and thus include the viewing of documentaries on: people with AIDS, people who got pregnant after having unprotected sex once, and the guy who got one blow job and now has herpes for life because there is no cure. **4.** a pretty easy A and actually sometimes really interesting, after all this is the one subject that is still relevant outside of school.

sick day (n) **1.** a break from school when a person feels physically ill. **2.** a break from school when a person doesn't want to go to class and is faking feeling physically ill. **3.** a day to watch lots of stupid game shows, surf the Net, IM friends in school, eat whatever one wants, and do other things one might not do if anyone else was home. **4.** a more fun day when you are actually *not* sick (throwing up all day is *not* better than going to school), but also harder to make happen.

slut (n) **1.** a girl who sees a lot of action with a lot of guys and is negatively judged as a result. **2.** in puritanical school environments, a girl who had sex with just one person and, oops, someone found out about it. **3.** a pretty girl, or one with well-developed breasts, who everyone is either hot for or jealous of and, thus, calls a "slut." **4.** when used loosely, a term that refers to a girl who flirts a lot. **5.** the female version of the player (who, due to an incredibly unfair double standard, is actually admired for engaging in precisely the same behavior).

S-T

smart (adj) **1.** a description for someone who has brains or who gets grades that make it seem like he or she has brains. **2.** an attribute that guides one in doing well on tests, kicking ass in **debates**, and not even having to **study** all that hard. **3.** genetically intelligent; some smart kids may actually get pretty bad grades or coast through **high school** with a C average (mostly because they are extremely bored), but then they go home and read James Joyce's *Ulysses* or Dante's *Inferno* in Italian to relax. *See also* **chess club** and **valedictorian**.

smoking (v) **1.** to suck toxic smoke from tobacco cigarettes into one's lungs. **2.** an activity done to seem **cool** or to rebel. **3.** something that comes with big costs: poor health, stinky breath, and, in the absolute worst case

scenario, nicotine addiction (or, you know, cancer). **4.** something most kids try at one point but hopefully realize right away just how nasty it is. *alternate use:* an expression used to refer to smoking marijuana (see **drugs**).

sneakers (n) **1.** shoes with rubber soles. **2.** accessories to an outfit that function as a huge fashion statement, and if even remotely high-end (never mind limited edition) cost more than a **parent's** monthly **car** payment. **3.** a potential boost to one's **cool** factor,

sneakers

but not if one is caught grooming them as if they're a champion thoroughbred, which some people do. **4.** the object of a total racket perpetrated by athletic shoe companies, which actually pay about $1.86 to produce each pair but spend millions of dollars on ad campaigns convincing people it's OK to blow loads of cash on a pair of shoes that (a) will be out of style next year and (b) get jacked pretty quickly. **5.** in some extreme cases, object of theft.

sophomores (n) **1.** students in their second year of high school and arguably the least stressed on campus because they are no longer the youngest in the school, and they don't have to worry about college yet. **2.** those who pick on freshmen solely because they are no longer the picked-on freshmen.

spelling bee (n) **1.** a competition in which smart, and often geeky, kids spell stuff. **2.** an intense competition (despite the fact that it merely involves kids standing on a stage spelling) whose participants will attempt to advance to city- and statewide contests, and possibly even the Scripps National Spelling Bee, which is broadcast on ESPN. **3.** a low-impact sport whose participants can be identified by an ever-present stack of flash cards and a complete inability to actually define any of the arcane, weird words they know how to spell.

standardized tests (n) **1.** evaluative exams (such as the SAT, ACT, and the NYC Regents exam) that are all the same, no matter the school. **2.** tests given to vast numbers of people in an effort to determine who's the "smartest" and which

S-T

schools are doing a good job and which ones are doing a bad job. **3.** annoying exams, which may end up dictating the kinds of classes one takes (honors, etc.) and the colleges one might gain admission to. **4.** total B.S. exams, which only prove how well one can cram for a test and are frequently biased toward certain types of learning and thinking. **5.** a staple of almost every school that ends up heavily influencing the curriculum, because many teachers are forced to spend half the semester teaching students how to pass the test rather than how to better understand the actual subject matter.

stoners (n) **1.** kids who smoke a lot of weed. **2.** kids who, in addition to number 1, communicate in that weird, tripped-out way that all stoners do and always seem fixated on food. **3.** kids who, in addition to number 1, might dress like a hippie or Bob Marley, but might also wear khakis and end up going to MIT.

straight edge (adj) **1.** a term to describe kids who make a lifestyle choice of not doing any kind of drugs or alcohol. **2.** a term used to give a cooler label to kids who espouse this philosophy (they are not "losers" but intentionally "straight edge"). **3.** kids who have already gone down the rabbit hole of addiction, and now don't touch anything that even hints of it. **4.** in some cases, kids who also forsake sex, smoking, meat, and even caffeine.

student government (n) **1.** the student-run council that supposedly helps govern a school; officers consist of the president, vice president, secretary, and treasurer. **2.** an association that allegedly has some impact on school life, though mainly only during the election itself, which is basically a popularity contest (after all, these people can't really introduce legislation such as "free candy all the time!" or "being late to class is OK!") **3.** something that looks pretty good on a college application.

studying (v) **1.** to try to memorize or at least grasp the information presented by a teacher in a class, or by some dry writer in a textbook. **2.** an activity that somehow usually manages to end up at the bottom of any To-do list. **3.** a good cover for going over to a friend's house and hanging out, or spending time with a boyfriend or girlfriend.

studying

substitute teacher (n) **1.** a teacher who has been called to cover a class for a sick colleague. **2.** a poor sap who must teach/look after students he or she does not know. **3.** the stand-in leader of a class, the appearance of which could mean a leisurely study hall (during which one can sleep or do any unfinished homework) or a pop quiz cruelly left behind by an absent teacher. **4.** an innocent, fearful, and professionally unstable human being who becomes the class' subject of torture.

S-T

suckup

suckup (n) **1.** a student who raises his or her hand in class all the time, always does the reading, and attempts to engage the teacher in high-minded conversations. **2.** a shameless, completely irritating, fawning student who asks questions specifically calculated to impress the teacher and who nonchalantly mentions the eight-DVD documentary he or she watched on the Crimean war over the weekend just for kicks. **3.** a straight-A student who still always does the extra credit. **4.** ironically, not always the teacher's pet, as some teachers clearly find all this behavior distasteful.

summer break (n) **1.** the months-long interval between the end of one school year and start of the next that always feels like it lasts about five seconds. **2.** a break that can include torrid romances, camp, family vacations, jobs, lots of parties, and the complete and total transformation of oneself (which usually lasts a few weeks into the new school year). **3.** a time during which it is possible to feel as if one has adopted a whole new reality, entirely separate from the daily grind of high school, until the crushing realization that you have to go back descends.

summer school (n) **1.** classes one must take over summer break, typically to keep one from being held back. **2.** the least desirable way to spend a summer. **3.** a way for smart kids to advance ahead of the rest of their class, and possibly graduate early.

S-T

Sweet 16

super senior (n) **1.** a student who is a senior for a second year after being held back. **2.** a student who has realized the true importance of showing up to gym class.

suspension (n) **1.** a punishment involving not being able to go to school for a certain period of time. **2.** a pretty severe sentence as far as school goes, because if one had just made a minor boo-boo, he or she would be in detention with all the other low-grade offenders who cut class.

Sweet 16 (n) **1.** the celebration of a girl's 16th birthday, which is considered a big milestone (though, if one really thinks about it, it's a completely random birthday because turning 16 doesn't allow drinking, voting, or even, in some cities, driving. **2.** for some people, a really big deal that may involve huge and expensive parties, bright and expensive dresses, fights between parents and daughters in regards to the parties and dresses, and oversized gifts (like new cars with big bows on them).

S-T

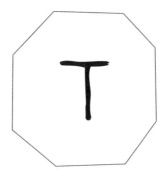

tattoos (n) **1.** permanent body art drawn into one's skin using needles. **2.** little and big paintings of red flowers, green tribal arm bands, and black Chinese characters (most often seen on people who are not Chinese) that without the help of lasers and lots and lots of money, will never, ever come off. **3.** decorations on the skin that seem really **cool** when people get them in October, but maybe not so cool when they're applying for a **job** the following June. **4.** in some cases, a declaration of someone's **love** for another, which is almost always a really bad idea.

tattoos

teacher (n) **1.** an instructor of semester-length courses on subjects like English, science, math, social studies, and sex ed. **2.** a person who knows a lot about the subject he or she is teaching. **3.** a person who knows nothing about the subject he or she is teaching but was hired anyway because of a teacher shortage. **4.** an old, tired person who has been teaching the same subject for 25 years and is kind of operating on autopilot. **5.** an adult who wields an enormous amount of power over students for at least half of the year, which ultimately involves various forms of torture, such as impossible homework assignments, pop quizzes, and final exams (the grades of which will result in raising or destroying one's GPA). **6.** a person who works ridiculously hard and is sorely underpaid but remains the envy of many adult friends because he or she can avoid dealing with corporate America and take whole summers off.

teacher's lounge (n) **1.** a room where teachers can escape from the insanity of high school. **2.** a depressing and kind of grungy room with ugly furniture where teachers eat, complain about the kids, and use all the swear words they prohibit the use of in class.

teacher's pet (n) **1.** a kid a teacher often likes more than everyone else. **2.** the sole goal of a suckup, though not always successfully accomplished. **3.** someone who is chosen, subconsciously, by the teacher because he or she is really smart, really interested in the subject matter, really hot, or simply reminds the teacher of himself or herself at that age.

S-T

text (n) **1.** a form of communication that is executed via cell phone. **2.** a message, the sending of which conveniently eliminates the need to punch in someone's number, wait for an answer, and respond with something dumb / funny / factual (U R gay, OMG JT is here). **3.** a type of communication that dispatches with the need to actually speak to other people. **4.** a helpful form of code, as even if parents scroll through texts, they won't have the slightest idea of how to go about translating them. **5.** somewhat of a waste of time, due to the fact that one can text back and forth with a friend for a very long time and say / learn absolutely nothing.

these are the best years of your life (exp) **1.** a platitude often spoken by parents, teachers, guidance counselors, and other adults. **2.** a total lie (thank goodness).

text

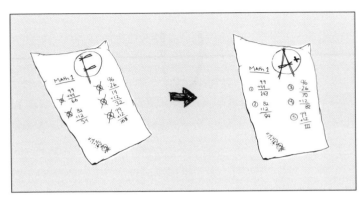

tutor

tutor (n) **1.** the person parents hire to help a kid do better in school because they think the kid is learning disabled or something (instead of just being bored or lazy), or they want the kid to go to a really good college and a B just isn't cutting it. **2.** reinforcements enlisted to help prepare a student for the SATs, in which case one has to do even more homework-type exercises that aren't even for school or going to get graded. **3.** a really hot upperclassman or college kid, if one is lucky, for whom one will actually do the required work in an effort to impress.

S-T

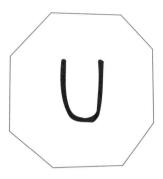

uniform (n) **1.** an outfit that students are required to wear at places like Catholic schools and very fancy private schools. **2.** for Catholic school students, clothing that may hail from Uniforms R Us, is made of nasty polyester, and will often incorporate some kind of muted plaid skirt for girls. **3.** for private school students, clothing that comes from places like Brooks Brothers and Saks Fifth Avenue, is made of fine merino wool and cashmere, and comes in hues of khaki, navy, and burgundy. **4.** a vehicle that squelches one of the few ways a student might be able to express oneself. **5.** an easy solution to the problem of what one is going to wear to school, which can be kind of nice, especially when running late.

uniform

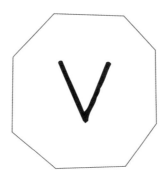

vacation (n) **1.** a glorious period of time without school; excluding summer break, the longest ones typically happen in late December and early spring. **2.** a time to shut down for a solid four or five days, unless some ruthless teacher has given assignments to do over the break. **3.** a good time to catch up on sleeping and TV watching, and be jetted off to Vail, or St. Tropez, or Paris by wealthy parents or a wealthy friend's family.

valedictorian (n) **1.** the person who gets selected to make a speech at graduation. **2.** the smartest person in a graduating class (or at least the one who knew what classes to take to get the highest GPA). **3.** a title for which winning is sort of a curse, because with it one is expected to cure cancer or write the next great American novel — or risk being forever seen as not living up to one's potential.

Valentine's Day (n) **1.** a day of "love." **2.** a horrible, depressing holiday for those not dating anyone, as they must endure the sight of people walking around with roses, balloons, and chocolates, and feel like an undesirable loser. **3.** also a lousy holiday for people with a boyfriend or girlfriend, since there's a ton of pressure involved and whatever gift you get/give is often disappointing in some way. **4.** a day during which unfulfilled fantasies of possibly having a secret admirer only add insult to injury. **5.** a day on which one or two pretty girls — who aren't dating anyone, by the way — will always get multiple roses from all the guys who have crushes on them, which will make all of the rejects talk about how much they hate Valentine's Day and how it should be banned.

varsity (n) **1.** the "real" sports teams at a school, with most team members representing the junior and senior class; freshmen and sophomores are typically relegated to junior varsity teams, unless they happen to be really good or really huge. **2.** the team that earns guys varsity jackets, which they can then let their girlfriends wear and look totally dwarfed in; this is a really retro tradition (total throwback to the '50s), but guys still do it, and girls still love it. **3.** the team that earns one a varsity letter, if one's school is into that sort of thing.

Valentine's Day

U-V

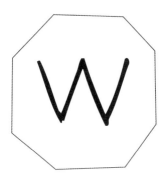

weekend (n) **1.** the two days a week when there is no school, i.e., Saturday and Sunday (though it really starts after the final bell on Friday). **2.** the weekly time slot for going to parties, hitting the mall, seeing bands, and going on dates. **3.** a time to do homework, though this is often the last priority. **4.** a brief vacation that ends on Sunday evening, which is the most depressing time of the entire week because of the realization that Monday is approaching.

SUNDAY	M	T	W	TH	F	SATURDAY

weekend

W

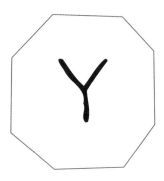

yearbook signing (n)
1. a tradition of passing yearbooks around for everyone to sign. **2.** a ritual that involves close friends and random people writing everything from extensive essays to a two-word "thought" (e.g., "love ya!") in one's yearbook. **3.** a weird competition (with whom, it's unclear), to see who can get the most people ever to sign their yearbook. **4.** an opportunity for seniors to write earnest sentiments to each other as though they are going off to war the next day and will never see one another again.

zits (n) See acne.

ACKNOWLEDGEMENTS

Thanks so much to the team at Orange Avenue Publishing: for the idea in the first place, for letting me do my thing, and for great editorial support. A special shout out to Publisher Hallie Warshaw and Editorial Director Karen Macklin. (You guys can always sit with me at the lunch table.) Additionally, enormous gratitude to the Orange Avenue Teen Advisory Board, which helped me keep it real.

Thanks to Ryan Baritot and Todd Kuchinski for responding to the call. A gold star to Dylan Gillett for his inspired, generous contributions, and for being as funny as he was in high school.

Of course, I'd be remiss if I didn't also thank all who trudged through high school with me. (East High represent!) A special nod to BH for providing the inspiration for "bitch."

And, of course, an extra special thanks to the Team Bergen cheerleaders: Jonah & Cuomo.

ABOUT
THE
AUTHOR

Lois Beckwith is a freelance writer based in Brooklyn, New York. She is also the author of *The Dictionary of Corporate Bullshit*.